All Scripture references taken from the KJV of the Holy Bible, unless otherwise indicated.

**The Wasters:** *Thieves of Darkness 2*
by Dr. Marlene Miles

Freshwater Press 2024
freshwaterpress9@gmail.com

ISBN: 978-1-963164-28-2

Paperback Version

Copyright 2024, Dr. Marlene Miles

All rights reserved. No part of this book may be reproduced, distributed, or transmitted by any means or in any means including photocopying, recording or other electronic or mechanical methods without prior written permission of the publisher except in the case of brief publications or critical reviews.

## Table of Contents

The Waster Spirit ............................................. 5
Those Hands ................................................. 11
Those Kids ................................................... 20
Wasting Wifey-ness ...................................... 23
It Takes Faith ............................................... 31
The Waster Won .......................................... 36
Let Purpose Work ........................................ 42
Actions of the Waster Spirit ........................ 49
Satan Seeking Permission ........................... 53
Those Who *Lunch* ...................................... 61
Prayers ........................................................ 64
This Draws the Wasters .............................. 66
How Is This Happening? .............................. 69
Signs of the Waster ..................................... 71
Get Delivered from the Waster Spirit: ........ 75
Waster Fire Prayers .................................... 78
Prayers Against Prosperity Wasters ........... 82
Fire of God .................................................. 84
In the Name of Jesus .................................. 87
Recovery: Take It Back ................................ 92
*Dear Reader* .............................................. 94
Other books by this author ........................ 95

# The Wasters

## *Thieves of Darkness 2*

And the waster shall come upon every city, that not a city shall escape; and the valley shall perish, and the plateau shall be destroyed: as Jehovah hath said.
Jeremiah 48:8

*(In the Scriptures the waster is also called the spoiler, plunderer, or destroyer, depending on Bible translation.)*

# The Waster Spirit

The *thieves of darkness* who come to steal from the saints of God are *emptiers, wasters, swallowers,* and *devourers.* The book, **The Emptiers: Thieves of Darkness** is the first of a series about the thieves from Satan's kingdom, what they are, how they work, how they get in, and how to get them out of your life.

There are several types of thieves that come to steal from men. The first written about is the *emptier spirit.* They will allow you to stay alive, but you will lose your money and financial stability. They will make you a slave to your job, a slave in your life, leaving you feeling washed up and hopeless, while you are still alive.

You can't serve God effectively with no money, no tithes, no offerings. If the devil knows that, why don't we? No, you shouldn't serve money; we serve God, but money has a place in everyone's life. We must make sure it is a godly place.

The second type of thief is the *waster*. These powers wait for you to labour or gather only to come and destroy your harvest (Judges 6:1-6). There are powers that come to attack your marriage, business, ministry, or children after you have labored to build them.

What is the *waster spirit?*
As we cannot see *spirits*, we know of their presence by the conditions on the ground. By the conditions in our flesh and in our physical lives we deduce what *spirits* are around or are in operation.

Some of the signs of the *waster spirit* working in your life are such as missing opportunities, missing chance after chance because something always happens that interferes with your success or your breakthrough.

You've been in relationships that should lead to marriage -- but something always happens. It may not be the same something, but then again it may. Things may be going along fine and then you fly off the handle one day because you have a temper problem. You tell the young man to go away, and he does. Only this time he stays away. In your foolish mind you thought it would make him want you more and then pursue you.

Nope.

A grown man found out that he had a 21-year-old son from a high school relationship. When he spoke to the woman he said, *"You moved away."* Then he asked her, *"Why didn't you tell me that you were pregnant?"*

She said, *"Yes, I moved, but you never came after me, did you?"*

He responded, *"I didn't know I was supposed to."* Pregnant or not, that man would have married that woman; he just never knew why she moved away. That woman would have had a husband, and that child would have had a father. Now that the young man is 21, the best he can hope for is friendship from the man that donated seed to his birth.

The woman wasted that child's chance to have a father in his childhood.

Another example of the waster is on a regular day you wake up late and quickly rush out of the house for work. You miss **every** light on the way to work if you are driving. That is a *waster spirit* in operation. It torments, steals, kills, and destroys.

The *spirit of the waster* wastes time, it wastes money, and it can waste people. You must take a strong position against it, or it will take a strong position against you. The *waster spirit* can attack a person to even keep them from going to their job.

Saints of God, just because you have received from God, you don't laze around on easy street because the wasters will still be on assignment to take it from you. It's one of the reasons why you don't advertise everything you have to the world. King Hezekiah showed off all his wealth to the men that came to basically *case* the palace, (Isaiah 39). He not only lost everything, but they were eventually taken into captivity. Stop showing off! Stop showing the world all your stuff. If you are in Christ, you should not have the need to boast.

Wasters will come and attack your business, your ministry, your family, your life after you've built it up. Once you get money you don't stop serving God, if you do, it smacks of now serving Mammon. Further, you will have no protection from

God if you stop serving Him, and Him alone. Wasters are ever on the prowl to try to take what you have. Do you think they only want to steal from poor people?

Even though I warn against broadcasting property online, the thief could be right there in your own house. This is not to make you paranoid; it is to make you discerning, aware, alert, and wise.

Other categories of thieves are the *swallowers* and the *devourers*. There is so much in our Bible about devourers that they need their own book.

Have no doubt, Satan is the *emptier*, the king of emptiers. Satan is the *waster*, he is the leader of all thieves of darkness; he comes to steal, kill, and destroy.

## Those Hands

There are so many people who say they want to save the planet, save the whales, save the ozone layer, save this, and save that. All those things need to be preserved **and** souls need to be saved. We each need to do the work of an evangelist, but evangelism most often takes money and resources. If the thief has ripped you off, that can negatively impact or ruin your life and ministry. This book is to help you defeat them, so they don't defeat you in your purpose in life.

I've seen many, even those who want to save the planet and near-extinct animals are themselves victims of the *waster spirit.* So many have careless hands, they have wasteful hands. That has irked me for so many years that I wrote a book on how not to be wasteful that applies to my own profession, dentistry.

In my profession and others, as well, those wasteful hands:

- Drop things.
- Break things.
- Misuse things.
- Use twice or three times as much as is needed.
- Throw good things into the trash bin.

Those wasteful hands spend extravagantly on food. How many of you have ever paid $40 for a $20 sandwich? Have you ever even looked into this? How much does it cost when you go to that restaurant versus how much it costs to order it online and have it delivered to your house or your office? How much does it cost in the restaurant vs the online price for delivery? Those prices are different.

The Covid Pandemic really set most of this exaggeration of prices and greed in motion. Perhaps it was need. Perhaps it wasn't; perhaps it was greed.

Logically, if you would lose $1000 to go get a sandwich, then paying a $10 delivery fee may be worth it. But if you are sitting around your house, DOING NOTHING and just don't *feel like* going to pick up your own sandwich—that is wasteful. *Feel like* is always expensive no matter what it applies to.

So, if you're hungry and willing to pay *whatever*, like Esau you will probably pay too much. If you're paying the devil for anything he did for you or promised, you are paying everything. Even what's in your bank account is not enough for the devil; he wants everything and even into your generations.

A man who is a lover of wisdom is a joy to his father: but he who goes in the company of loose women is a waster of wealth. (Prov 29:3)

God hates the wasting of wealth. Look at the numbers. You could be wasting wealth or money that is not pleasing to God, your wallet, your bank account, or your future.

Go to the kitchen and make your own sandwich or go to the restaurant and pick it up yourself.

He also that is slothful in his work is brother to him that is a great waster. (Prov 18:9)

Another sign of the *waster* in action is when your hard work doesn't turn in to what you thought it would or should. You feel like you are always losing money. Even when God answers financial prayers, one bad thing after another happens. It seems that when you have money there comes a cascade of bad things to drain you of that money. That is the work of the *waster*.

God is into wise stewardship; it is one of the reasons man was put on Earth. God loved Joseph because he was prudent; Joseph was a wise steward.

Before we leave this chapter, lets pray for the hands. Father, I've been bound for a long time, I need liberty, in the Name of Jesus. Free me, Lord, by Your power, by Your Grace, in the Name of Jesus.

With feeble hands, or weak hands, you can be easily ripped off by the enemy. Have you seen this in your dreams? When you are being ripped off in your dreams, that is the forerunner to what the enemy wants to do to you in the natural, and if demonic dreams are not prayer treated, that is exactly what will happen to you in real life.

Lord, remove the spiritual chains from my hands, in the Name of Jesus.

Lord, place Fire in my hands, break chains on my hands, remove evil afflictions from my hands, in the Name of Jesus.

*Spirit of poverty* on my hands, Go! Go! Go!, in the Name of Jesus.

Lord, break every curse of bewitched hands, in the Name of Jesus.

Slavery curse on my hands, be broken. My hands, be free, be free, be free, in the Name of Jesus.

The curse of empty hands, barren hands be broken today by the power in the Blood of Jesus.

*(Above prayer points were adapted from Apostle Rodney Chipoyera.)*
https://www.youtube.com/@kpmtv235

Satanically padlocked hands, are hands that should be free to do the will of God, replenish the Earth, and to be fruitful and prosper. Chains or ropes tying my hands, any hands that are bound, break free, in the Name of Jesus.

Lord, I repent for every evil covenant in my bloodline that introduced spiritual padlocks, I renounce it; I denounce it, in the Name of Jesus.

Every spiritual padlock locking up the works of my hand, I send Thunder Fire; crumble and burn to ashes, in the Name of Jesus.

Curses spoken over my life, public or private, be broken along with the evil covenant that allowed the curse, in the Name of Jesus.

Any evil food that I have consumed in the natural or in the dream, I vomit it up, in the Name of Jesus.

Whatever the enemy is using to lock my hands, destiny, or future, catch Fire, in the Name of Jesus.

Every padlock used to lock away finances and prosperity from my life, catch Fire, and burn to ashes, in the Name of Jesus.

Satanic padlocks put on my hands, break and shatter by the power in the Blood of Jesus, in the Name of Jesus.

I renounce witchcraft powers, occultic powers, marine powers, ancestral powers behind any padlocks over my hands, in the Name of Jesus – break and let my hands go, in the Name of Jesus.

*(Above prayer points were adapted from Apostle Paul Williams,* https://www.youtube.com/watch?v=10uQBTbC4-w&t=469s *)*

Every generational covenant that has sentenced my hands to death, break today, in the Name of Jesus.

Every satanic glove and cover preventing my hands from prosperity, catch Fire.

Wasteful hands, feeble hands, weak hands, be strengthened by the Spirit of God, in the Name of Jesus.

Dead hands, be resurrected, in the Name of Jesus.

Satanic holes wasting fortune and investments of glory, be sealed by the power in the Blood of Jesus.

*Spirit of death* on my hands, be consumed by Fire, in the Name of Jesus.

Every power sent to stagnate my work and waste destiny, fail against me, in the Name of Jesus.

Every power against my hands to make me fail in projects and life, die, in the Name of Jesus.

Every arrow of the enemy in my hand, wasting all my opportunities in life, catch Fire and come out, in Jesus' Name.

Every financial frustration occurring in my hands, stop now, in the Name of Jesus.

Curses of abandoned projects, resurrect today, in the Name of Jesus.

Prosperous relationships ended because of dead or cursed hands be resurrected, now, in Jesus' Name.

Anointing of God, rest upon my hands now, and move my life forward in the Name of Jesus.

Lord, strengthen my hands today and give me Grace to prosper and not to waste or be wasted, in the Name of Jesus.

*(Above prayer points were adapted from James Akanbi, **Waste Them by Thunder 3**  
https://a.co/d/3UTVLBp )*

## Those Kids

- Powers that have vowed to waste the fruit of my labour, or the fruit of my loins, die, in Jesus' Name.

The *wasters* come to waste your life. They want to drain your resources and successes. Sometimes and somehow, they can influence you to waste your own resources and life.

Some people waste by throwing good money after bad, wasting it on children, relatives, or other people they know who are always asking for a handout and will never change. Parents have such a difficult job sometimes. They pour out and pour out for their own children, even that one who doesn't seem serious about life. Of course, that person could be infested with any of the thieving *spirits* of darkness, and if no one knows it, nobody can help them if the real problem isn't diagnosed or addressed, spiritually.

Sometimes, through pride or the fear of shame, parents keep helping the one child that is draining their resources trying to help that child finally become a success at something. Yes, for the sake of the child, but sometimes it is the parent that doesn't want to be embarrassed. That parent may have 2 or 3 other kids who are doing well, and one ne-er-do-well.

Instead of blindly cursing that child telling him or her that they will never amount to anything, help them, but help them spiritually. First and foremost, repent. Yes parents, you repent. Many times, what is in your child came either from you or through your bloodline. If they are being oppressed by a *waster spirit* it may be because of ancestral iniquity, and by the Grace of God it skipped you and maybe your other children.

It could be that the child is sent as your tormenter because you are in unforgiveness about something that the child knows nothing about. The kid may not even know why things work out the way they do in his or her life; they just know that they are frustrated. While all you just know is that they are frustrating you.

Are your children saved? All of them? Or is Christianity only for you and your spouse, and you haven't bothered to introduce Jesus to your children?

# Wasting Wifey-ness

Women, stop wasting your wifey-ness on someone you're not married to. Are you auditioning for the position, or have you made yourself believe you have it, already? GOD HATES that; He hates SIN: if you're giving away wifey-ness you are in sin because of what you're giving away. The recipient of such benevolence will probably never stop you from giving him what a husband should get, without being your husband.

And the waster shall come upon every city, that not a city shall escape; and the valley shall perish, and the plateau shall be destroyed: as Jehovah hath said.
(Jeremiah 48:8)

God will allow the wasters if you are in chronic sin.

> For the waster has come on her, even on Babylon, and her men of war are taken, their bows are broken: for the Lord is a rewarding God, and he will certainly give payment. (Jeremiah 51:56)

There are many kinds of wasters. Financial wasters are obvious. Stephen Darby spoke of the Grace *wasters* who are unsaved people, usually, but sometimes they are saved, but they are people who will not make the investment in their relationship with God and their spiritual life, but want to live off of *your* Grace.
https://www.youtube.com/watch?v=1sOFSmMapeg

There are time wasters, glory wasters and education *wasters*. Don't waste your own education. You are having fun at college on your parents' dime. You may procrastinate by saying that you can't decide what to be in life, what to major in. You are wasting time and money. Or maybe you are afraid to get out there and be an adult. Fear can waste time, resources, and your parents' patience, careers and even lives. Other types of wasters are:

- Marriage wasters.
- Anointing wasters.
- Health wasters.
- Youth can be wasted.
- Friendships can be wasted.
- Opportunity wasters.
- Time wasters.

Why do they say that getting drunk or drugged up is getting *wasted*? Because without right thinking and a clear mind the *spirit* of the *waster* can have his way in your life.

Regarding money, many people, even your own kids, may think they need **more** money. Some do need money; they don't have any money. But many need *money management*.

The ability to deal successfully with money takes **power**, and that power is from God. Money is spiritual, so money management begins in the spirit. From God, we get the power to get wealth, and the power to **keep** wealth. we need the devourer rebuked, we need the *emptiers* scattered and the *wasters* removed from our lives, off of our money, and other valuable resources, in the Name of Jesus.

It takes power not to become wasted, and that is the power of *No*. Being able to say *No* takes will power. Getting wasted takes your power from you.

The *spirit of the waster* is determined to WASTE whatever you've been given. Whatever you have amassed, created, or accumulated is at risk because the waster's greedy eyes are on your stuff.

You've seen it so many times in the natural with athletes, celebrities, and lottery winners who get a lot of money quickly, then mysteriously they don't have it any longer. They need to handle money spiritually, first.

Some say, *Easy come, easy go*—but it is the *spirit of the waster* in people's money. Those with a lackadaisical attitude such as, *here today, gone tomorrow* are easy subjects for the Thieves of Darkness.

Having your good things wasted or wasting it yourself happens too frequently. The Prodigal Son got his inheritance while his father was still alive. He left home and wasted it by living the party life. Don't let that happen to you; be wise in your stewardship of money, but don't worship money.

I've seen this *waster spirit* in action many times. I may be doing something kind for someone, but they push back on me, as if I'm doing something *to* them. But I'm really trying to do something **for** them. They are acting all kinds of weird and wrong. They seem frustrated and are frustrating me, too. Were it not for the Word of God, the voice of God, the Spirit of God telling me to keep doing something nice for them, I'd probably stop.

The *waster spirit* often travels with *pride* where a person may need something, but they will act as though they don't because they are so proud. They end up doing without something that was being given to them. That is a wasted opportunity, or a wasted blessing, depending on how you look at it.

A woman gave nice gifts to each of her three sisters for Christmas; but they each rejected their gift and became angry at that sister, probably because she was *able* to give them such a nice gift. *Jealousy, hatred,* and the *bitterness spirits* often travel with the *waster spirit*. Yes, the women wasted receiving a lovely gift, but worse, they rejected **relationship**.

By their own hand, they are ruining their own blessings by pushing people away from them because they cannot clearly see what is going on. That is how the *waster spirit* affects people.

Those right on the edge of being blessed, or at the brink of success or breakthrough, may have been so defeated or attacked by the enemy so many times that they don't recognize when something good is happening to them. They say it's darkest before dawn. Don't let the thieves of darkness encroach upon and steal your blessings right before the dawn of your breakthrough, which may be tomorrow morning.

To help those I'm helping, I'm the type to say, *"I'm about to bless you right now, what are you doing? Are you serious right now? You need to chill out."* My goal is always to leave people better than when I found them, because that's what I'd want people to do for me. But maybe, these people are not used to people like that around them and they become defensive.

Once, a so-called man of God to told me off for doing something nice for him and his ministry, AT NO CHARGE, and no strings attached. He asked why I did that, stating he has *people* to do that for him. My gift was totally, loudly, rudely rejected.

## It Takes Faith

It takes **faith** to expect better things for yourself. It takes faith to think that people are going to treat you well, or very well. Some things take time. Transitioning from no faith to faith, and then escalating to strong faith, takes time. We do not serve an Insta-God. A lot of what God is doing, and a lot of what God can do for you depends on your faith.

**Let faith have its perfect work.**

Pray to the Lord that your discernment is made strong, else, some people may end up blaming others for their predicaments when they should have faced the demon of the *wasters* responsible for their problems.

When the boss goes on vacation and gives you a temporary assignment to manage the place while he's gone-- he's not <u>*using*</u> you, but he is seeing what you can do. Your promotion is most likely at hand. Either that boss will promote you or at least increase you. Your taking more responsibility will add to your resume. God may have a promotion or an increase for you. GOD may be planning to promote you to another position, job, or even move you to another company.

But you have to discern, *Is this a waste of my time? Is this the **waster** spirit? Am I being used, or is this an opportunity?*

So, everything you do, do as unto the Lord.

Unless you are seriously under employed, how do you plan to get promoted without new skills, new tests, more training, and a way to show your ability, to show what you can do? This could be your chance.

One of the strategies of the *wasters* is to prevent people from recognizing opportunities. An amazing opportunity could look like the very opposite of what it is. The process may sometimes look like they are being *used*. It may look like *nothing* to them – they can't see it if it must be seen spiritually, if they are not spiritual.

These hidden chances look like setbacks or failures. Or it could look like people are using you and you're doing *their* job, and they make *waaaay* more money than you do. The situation may be disguised as something else and make people waste their own lives when they miss opportunities that can never be repeated. Some may be declaring, *I'm so tired of those people using me!!!* mumbling, grumbling, and resisting the "extra work with no pay." When a *waster spirit* is running that man, that man will run away from an opportunity rather than see it, run to it, or step into that possibility of promotion.

The *waster* desires you get demoted, not promoted. The waster doesn't even want you to stay the same, but he wants you to have less than you already have, down to nothing. So, the *waster spirit* may have you decide that you're not going to do that job--, how dare they, or you may be thinking to do *that* is beneath you.

The person who is not afflicted by this *spirit* may say, *I'm going to do this job as unto the Lord. I'm going to do this job that my boss asked me to do while he's on vacation in the Bahamas.* So, you step into the position and fulfill your promise. When the boss gets back there is commendation, a promotion, a bonus, a raise, or something good in it for you.

Alternatively, you may choose not to stand in for the boss. You only went to work 2 of those 5 days while the boss was gone. So, when he gets back, you get fired. You went from opportunity to a demotion. The *waster spirit* won that round.

Now what? Look for a new job, with a bad work history? That is worse than having to look for a new job or *choosing* to look for a new job.

- Anything that wants to downgrade me or squander my blessings is a *waster;* *s*pirit of the *waster*, be bound, and cast out of my life and finances, in the Name of Jesus.

## The Waster Won

A woman gets a new job with a title and a nice salary, in her field. It's the best job she's ever had. First time she's ever had it this good. Here comes the *waster.* Here is some of what happened in a short period of time.

- The first day of the job and the interview process was glorious.
- The second day and days after she arrived in the parking lot each morning in a haze of vape smoke that would either choke or impress Cheech & Chong.
- Her junior high school aged kid gets sick the third day of the job. Allegedly he needs surgery.

- Her car breaks down twice, at the end of the first week; one of those times it keeps her from coming to work.

(This is a side note, but I've noticed that employees seem to have trouble with their vehicles in a way that makes them late for work in the mornings. Not one of them has ever worried that their vehicle will not start up or take them home at the end of the day. Why do you think that is?)

- Later that week she gets into a shouting match with another employee over money missing from the first employee's purse.
- The first weekend after starting the job, she and her boyfriend get into an altercation with each other, and she has to go to court.
- She had to be sent home early the day that fight was reported because of making absolutely no sense for the first hour of the workday. She also smelled of alcohol. Perhaps it

was because of the fight and staying up all night?

- The second week there's a death in the family, very unexpected. Suddenly, the same day, the same hour of the death, she states she's a foster parent to the just-orphaned teen who still has another living parent who is alive and well, and no wills have been read or executed.
- The third week an unknown man whom she describes as her *brother*, comes into the establishment demanding to see her. He states that he came by, **from out of state**, to give her money because she has no money for gas. It is further revealed that he has to go right back where he is from because his mother had died of Covid, even before he had left that other state, yet this man is out and about, wearing no mask in business establishments.

- She didn't make it to the fourth week; it's just too much. Too much drama. Too much everything.

Whether she's cooperating with the *waster spirit* by her own sin, such as her over the top excuses for not coming to work, family iniquity, or other curses, it's still an open door for the *waster*. Is the waster doing her in, or has she invited and allowed this *waster* for so long that it has taken up residence in her soul and just runs every good thing she gets into the ground.

Of a fact, discord propagates poverty, and we can clearly see how that woman's chaotic life is full of arguments and fights. For this reason, the *waster spirit* has a welcome mat, 24/7.

- By the power of the God of Elijah, let all wasters in my life be wasted, in the Name of Jesus.

She didn't make it to week 4 of that new job with the title, position, and benefits because the *spirit* of the *waster* won. That *spirit* defeated her and took her breakthrough job, her breakthrough opportunity for her and her family.

Under the *spirit* of the *waster* there is no real progress in life. You are still in the same position and job where you first started, if you even have a job.

You have no promotion. Even when people try to help you, somehow that *spirit* makes you push those people away, along with their offers and opportunities. This leaves a person oppressed by or possessed of the *waster spirit*. This leaves a person always at square one, or as I like to say, square zero.

With the *waster spirit*, you work for people who *have*. They have money, means and success, but you *have not*. You or your household suffer repeated illnesses and sicknesses. You help others, but when will someone help **you**?

You keep missing destiny appointments and divine connections--, it's like being in the wrong place at the wrong time, all the time.

- Any *spirit* or power that is causing me to ruin my own life by my hand, die, in the Name of Jesus.

## Let Purpose Work

No weapon formed against you shall prosper,
And every tongue *which* rises against you in judgment you shall condemn.
This *is* the heritage of the servants of the LORD,
And their righteousness *is* from Me,"
Says the LORD. (Isaiah 54:17)

Saints of God: What are you doing in life? What are you *supposed* to be doing? If you don't know--- then the *waster* is already at work. What is your divine purpose? Don't blame others if you don't know. You need to know. Blaming others because you don't know won't get you anywhere. The only way out is to fight and defeat any *spirit* that is blocking you, stealing from you, lying to you, and is not supposed to be in your life in the first place.

A lot of folks are being wasted every day because they never find out what God wants them to do. They may be living their best life, their entertainment life, their party life: womanizing, man chasing, smoking, drinking, and out all night, throwing their lives away. All that can lead to destruction, disaster, demotion, and downgrades in life. They might as well look out for:

- -accidental pregnancy.
- -no spouse
- -wrong spouse
- - being weighed down by life
- - being oppressed and depressed.

Sometimes whole families are wasted by collective captivity.

Speaking of spouses, here's another example of the *waster* at work: Elizabeth Taylor got married 8 times. She married one of the men, Richard Burton--, twice. (God hates that). Going from one man to the next, from one woman to the next--, serial dating, ritual sex--, all that is work of the *waster spirit.*

The Israelites wasted all the opportunities to hear and obey the Lord to make it into the Promised Land. While doing so there was idolatry and orgies involved. They wasted that opportunity, that blessing, and 40 years in the Wilderness.

Esau wasted all his opportunities.

Some are wasting their talents--, using them to glorify the devil, or glorify the world, versus how God intended they use those gifts.

- Some are attacked by evil powers that can exchange or steal virtues.
- Others, by deception, bury their own talents and gifts. Some do it willingly by trying to get something for nothing or making devil deals.

- Some do it by mistake, never intending to make devil deals. Still, sin has consequences.
- Burying one's talent as we have learned from the Parable of the Talent will cause that person to be labeled as *unprofitable.*

"You gave me one talent and since I did not see you and because I was afraid, and know that you wanted to reap where you did not sow, I buried it." Said the man with one talent.

The master had no other option but to throw him into outer darkness where there is weeping and gnashing of teeth.
(Matthew 25:29-30)

Sounds like hell, doesn't it? Don't bury your talents. You will have to give an account of your talents, your actions, and even your words. Just as that man came back for a report on those talents, so we will have to tell God what we did with what He gave us.

Satan can waste a person's talents and health by keeping the person on a job that wastes his or her time, health, energy, and abilities. The devil can delay good things hoped for and make the heart sick.

You can waste anything but the most egregious thing to waste is your life.

You must stop the *wasters* up against your life right now. If they have already wasted anything in your life, surely you don't want to lose anything else.

Before you were born, God had a purpose for you and a plan. If you are not fulfilling that purpose, your destiny is in danger, your life could be in danger, because walking in **Purpose** protects your life, it protects your destiny. When you are in God's timeline, you are safe; when you're out of it--, when you are in the devil's timeline, you are in every danger.

The name of the Lord is a strong tower,
the righteous run in and they are safe.
(Proverbs 18:10)

No matter what your position is in the *church*, if you are not in your right position in the Kingdom of God, then the *waster* has been at work in your life. Are you IN Jesus' Christ?

False prophets and false pastors are famous for holding people back from ministry, usually because of jealousy of the spiritual gifts and anointing of the up and coming. Church hurt doesn't just come from or through the pews, it can come from the pulpit.

Cursed be he that doeth the work of the LORD deceitfully, (Jeremiah 48:10a)

While we are careful not to embrace a *spirit of offense*, we must discern when we are falling under conviction by the Holy Spirit and not blame anyone who may be telling us the truth, that we may not want to hear. Offense is a great waster. It will drive a person away from their blessing instead of toward it.

Break yourself loose from the *waster spirit*, or before you know it you may be asking yourself, Where have the years gone? *Wasters* are notorious for wasting time and causing people to waste time. The purpose of a wasted life is to torment you, to mock God, to mock you. It is to torment you. At the end you may be asking, *Where did the time go? What have I accomplished in my life?* It is very disheartening if it has all been taken from you. It's why the Ecclesiastical preacher is crying, *Vanity, vanity, all is vanity.*

Don't let that be you. Pray to God, listen to God, He is the same One who called you, He knows what purpose and what gifts He put in you; let Him fully lead you. Amen.

If you haven't been working for God, then by default, you have been working for the devil. Dedicate, or rededicate your talents and gifts to the Lord, and to the Kingdom and get busy doing your Purpose.

## Actions of the Waster Spirit

The Israelites did evil in the LORD's sight. So, the LORD handed them over to the Midianites for seven years. The Midianites were so cruel that the Israelites made hiding places for themselves in the mountains, caves, and strongholds. Whenever the Israelites planted their crops, marauders from Midian, Amalek, and the people of the east would attack Israel,

camping in the land and destroying crops as far away as Gaza. They left the Israelites with nothing to eat, taking all the sheep, goats, cattle, and donkeys.

These enemy hordes, coming with their livestock and tents, were as thick as locusts; they arrived on droves of camels too numerous to count. And they stayed until the land was stripped bare.

So Israel was reduced to starvation by the Midianites. Then the Israelites cried out to the LORD for help.
(Judges 6:1-6)

- By the God of Elijah, let all the *wasters* in my life be wasted, in the Name of Jesus.

Under the *spirit of the waster* in addition to what was mentioned earlier,

- You sow but do you reap?
- Others get promoted, but where is your promotion?
- Rise and fall.
- Chaos.
- Work a lot, but enjoy a little.
- Repeated problems.
- Life is getting harder instead of easier.
- Missing appointments, and divine connections.

Lord, in the Name of Jesus, let every wasting strongman assigned against me, die, in the Name of Jesus.

- Sudden disfavor and reproach.
- Destruction of, or you destroying things that will bring you profit.

- Being blocked from places where you can get deliverance.

Look how long this list is; having the *waster spirit* in your life is horrible. The devil wants to waste a person's entire life, not just their resources, although he starts there.

*Wasted* in the Bible:

- Lot's wife was **wasted**.
- Reuben, the first born of Judah wasted that position, or he was *wasted* by the *waster spirit*.
- Achan wasted the opportunity to tap into the power of giving to God. Achan became wasted by God.
- Eli's sons **wasted** their positions and were then ultimately wasted.
- Saul **wasted** position, kingship, and God's anointing by sins of disobedience, and seeking witches.

The *waster* is in action if you are living beneath God's plan for your life, actually, that means the *waster* is winning when there is attack after attack.

Participating in serial sex is a sign of a *waster* in a life. In the natural many men will celebrate other men who do this calling them **players**. When women do this they are called nympho's and worse. Professional people call this sex addiction, but there is at least one evil *spirit* that has lodged in the soul and life of its victim. Tiger Woods, and others look like **players**, but they are wasting seed because the *spirit of the waster* is in full effect in their lives. They are wasting opportunities for God to bring righteous seed to the Earth.

Because of evil covenants, curses may be coming at you. These covenants may be your fault and others may be ancestral in origin.

Wasters are like locusts; they eat up everything. Just like the Midianites and the Amalekites were tearing up all the Israelites' crops, as in Judges 6.

- Any power out to waste me, Lord, waste that power, in Jesus' Name.

## Satan Seeking Permission

Satan is a waster, _the_ waster. When anyone breaks the Laws of God, Satan will appear before the Throne of God **to seek permission to *waste*** that person, that is, at least attack them, with the intention of doing them in either quickly or slowly. Satan wants to do as much damage as possible to any man.

My book, ***Evil Petition*** https://a.co/d/2IFRhpG. tells how the devil has to get permission, and has to stand on legal ground to afflict or to waste lives, resources, marriages, homes, and anything else he can find to tear up. That book also has prayers to help you answer and overcome *evil petition* in the Courts of Heaven.

When the *waster* is in your life, you may experience multiple unexplained failures in any or every aspect of your life, such as relationships, financial failures, ministry failures, health failures. After you have worked hard for something, the *waster* is sent into your life to keep you from actually getting what you've worked for.

Gifts, talents, skills, abilities, resources that you could be using, for some reason or other, you can't use. It could be because you don't know how to use them, or the opportunity to use them is blocked from you.

You're smart, *right*? Yeah, you're smart, and what are you doing with that intelligence, with all that smartness? What are you doing with that gift? That opportunity is blocked for you to use your mind to bring glory to God.

My mother was a nutritionist for the state prison system. She often told us that most of the inmates in that prison were very smart people. She pondered that they may be among the smartest people.

Recall when Israel was captured by Babylon, they chose the young, the brightest and the best. They chose those with something on the ball, like Daniel, Shadrach, Meshach, and Abednego. Folks, that's who the devil comes for. It's why you hear people say that a life is wasted, or that a person wasted their life or wasted their opportunities, or a gift, talent or skill. It's because the devil came for them and wasted them.

Putting a young person in prison, even though they may have deserved it because they wouldn't learn any other way is the penal system playing right into Satan's plan--, to lock up and block up the brightest and the best.

Back to my mother's observation: She stated that those inmates were so smart, but their problem was that they thought they were smarter than everyone else. Criminals often think like that.

Is that not pride?

The *spirit of pride* is a waster. Case in point. We can clearly see when the youth is incarcerated for many years or even life--, he or she wasn't emptied, they still had their gifts. Joseph still had his gifts in Potiphar's house and in the prison. He was actually using those gifts, but he was in prison, wasting away.

We can surmise that all sin and especially works of the flesh are wasters and will waste a life.

Valuable resources are untapped, unused. You are not using the resources that could be making you financially sound, healthy, wealthy, married-, whatever you are lacking. The *waster spirit* is the cause of all of that.

You may have been attracting or hanging out with the wrong crowd. What am I saying?-- *you* may **be** the wrong crowd. Stop blaming others all the time; **you** could be your whole problem if the *waster spirit* is fully embedded into your life. Ask God. Pray. Always be prayerful.

The *waster spirit* makes you misuse or not use the gifts that God has placed in you. As discussed, your gifts may be buried. Your star may be buried. Your destiny could be buried or covered, either spiritually or in the case of being locked away somewhere, physically.

Even if a person is not imprisoned, *waster spirit* attacks may be so severe or so frequent that they may frustrate you to the degree that you will begin to believe that nothing good can happen in your life. You may begin to think that good things and nice things are for others and not for you.

This will do major damage to your faith in God.

Unrepented sin, of any kind, is the primary way the door is open to the devil, the *emptier*, the *waster*, the *swallower*, the *devourer,* leaving you open for attack.

- Prayerless/carelessness
- Robbing God in tithes and offerings.

Please know that when you rob God in tithes and offerings you are also robbing yourself. It is like embezzlement from your own company. Why? Because you belong to God. As you are part of the Kingdom and you are heir to the Kingdom--, when you don't, tithe, you rob God and yourself.

And, your tithes and offerings are sacrifices for the Godly altar that is making your life what it is, and in many cases fighting the evil altars that may be emanating against you and your bloodline. Nothing on the altar from you, your family or your bloodline diminishes the power to fight the altars that are speaking against you. Believe me, there are altars speaking against you; some of them ancient that you know nothing about.

- Evil dedication.

- Demonic covenants/ancestral/evil foundation.

REPENT. If you're saved, repent. If you are not saved, get saved, and repent.

And I will restore to you the years which the swarming locust has eaten, the locust larvae, and the stripping locust, and the cutting locust, My great army which I sent among you.' And you shall eat in plenty, and be satisfied, and praise the name of Jehovah your God, who has dealt with you wonderfully; and **My people shall never be ashamed.**
(Joel 2:25, 26)

Locusts eat everything in sight, they destroy crops; they are wasters.

The wasters come to destroy crops that are not in your hand yet, but you have put considerable work into planting, cultivating, and tending to it. It is not the seed, when you're at the beginning of the process, it is the CROP. The seed has sprouted and grown up and it is about to bear fruit; it is a whole crop. You have hope, expectation, you have needs and plans – here comes the *waster spirit,* like a locust to devour it and eat it all up.

It's like getting to your senior year in college and never finishing your last 3 credit hours. Or, it is like not being able to pay the last of your school fees and you've finished all that coursework, so that you can receive your diploma or certificate.
All that time, all that work, all that labor, but where is your reward?

## Those Who *Lunch*

*To waste* means to use incorrectly or in a wrong, inefficient, or ungodly way. You may have a gift, skill, talent, or ability but either it's not working as it should, or you are not working it, for any reason.

Not using something to its top efficiency is wasteful. A woman who earned multiple degrees became a medical doctor. Finally, an eligible man proposed to her. As the wedding date approached, she found out that her intended husband wanted her to stay home, clean the house, and cook his meals. He let her know that he doesn't want her to drive, listen to music, or watch television. That's it. That's what he wanted her to do; actually, the longer list was all the things he *didn't* want her to do.

She didn't marry him.

Could this be why women who lunch--, *lunch?* They are bored and not challenged. Even if they don't become desperate housewives, they are still wasting gifts, talents, skills, abilities, and in the above case, education. This woman is a world traveler, she has boldly gone to multiple continents and countries even as a solo traveler. She has completed a medical degree and has friends all over the world. For someone to tell her that she can only stay home and cook and clean, which, by the way, she is not good at either, is like telling her she'll be going to prison. Seriously, what a waste.

If the person was supposed to have gone to college, get a degree, and travel the world but did not, whether they got married or not it is still disobedience and failed assignment to purpose. It doesn't matter who or what stopped purpose it is still a failure.

To waste is to render something useless. Not mixing faith with the Word of God is a waste. Faith without works is dead; and that's a waste. Mixing the Word of God with tradition makes the Word of no effect; that is waste.

Ultimately, to waste is to make something completely unusable and useless.

- Lord, forgive me for all that I have wasted in my life, in the Name of Jesus.
- Forgive me for not using everything You've given me, Lord, to the maximum.

Don't be a waster, saints of God. Don't be idle. Use everything to its fullest capacity, to the glory of God.

To be delivered from this, you must be saved. You need the Holy Spirit and do violent warfare. Repent of every sin, both known and unknown, and engage in spiritual warfare--, and mean it.

## Prayers

Father, arrest every plan the wasters have planned against me. I command those plans to perish by Fire, in Jesus' Name.

Father, arise and let all household wasters scatter, by the power in the Blood of Jesus.

Father, arise and dismantle all curses, spells, declarations, and incantations of the wasters over my life, in Jesus' Name.

I repent of all of my sins. Let every evil covenant be broken, in the Name of Jesus.

I command every door the wasters have been using to access my life to be slammed shut by the angels of God, and sealed by the Blood of Jesus, in Jesus' Name.

## This Draws the Wasters

The following things bring the *waster* into a life.

Unrepentant sin such as fornication, adultery or other sex sins. All works of the flesh wastes God's plan for my life.

Evil human agents, false prophets, witches, warlocks, satanists and compromised preachers who don't even preach deliverance or spiritual warfare. Some are ignorant of the devil's devices and determined that they are not. Some are not ignorant of the devil's devices but are on assignment. Some don't teach it, because their ears are closed, and they cannot hear new things. If the Holy Spirit is not in them, they cannot hear Truth.

Those who think that everything there is to know about God has already been revealed are sorely mistaken. Not only that, but some also believe that if God doesn't tell them, and *only* them, then it is not truth. They behave as if they are the only ones saved.

With a heart of compassion those who have suffered or been through a thing will surely be able to hear God tell them what has afflicted them, especially if they are crying out to God to ask both why, and what to do about it.

Some are restrained from teaching spiritual warfare or deliverance. They can't speak against it if they are *compromised*, spiritually.

The devil has a greater plan than one-on-one evil that people do to one another. The devil desires that folks are led astray and that as many lives as possible are wasted--, even Christian lives. Therefore, we must discern every *spirit*.

Seeing your life, and good things in your life perish before your very eyes is tormenting, and devastating. How many have cried out, *This is not what I signed up for?* Or, *This can't be my real life!*

The wasters can be the cause all this loss and suffering.

## How Is This Happening?

The *waster spirit* can work through people via multiple avenues. You could be one of those people who is self-sabotaging your own successes. You can waste your own life.

People waste their own lives by bad habits, addictions, bad relationships, lack of discipline. The enemy can cause you in jest, or folly to speak curses upon your own life, destiny, or blessings. If Jospeh could have learned this: Keep your mouth shut. Keep plans to yourself and ask the Lord who you can share your plans with before doing so.

The enemy can waste your life; the devil can waste your life. *The devil himself can waste you*: (1 Peter 5:8). The devil must *seek* whom he can devour. Finish and finish well. Start and finish in season, else that leaves an open door for enemy waster attack.

The enemy can waste people through other people who may be evil, or they may be ignorant and working for the devil *blindly*. People can be on assignment to speak a curse over you before you can barely get started in life. Your own parent, sibling friend, relative, or fake friend can be on that assignment.

God can waste you if you hatefully, and knowingly, chronically refuse to obey the Lord, God will waste you. Onan had an assignment to impregnate Tamar; he spilled the seed instead. Eli's sons, Hophni and Phineas had sex with the temple prostitutes. God struck them down. (2 Samuel 2:22). Nadab and Abihu offered strange fire before the Lord; God wasted them, (Leviticus 10).

God is not playing.

## Signs of the Waster

*List from: Warnings from God of Waster Spirits,* (Dr. D. K. Olukoya, MFM Ministries)

- Eating in the dream.
- Filled with lust and sexual sin.
- Addictions.
- Reproach is on you.
- Dry prayer life, prayerless, careless.

Folks, the devil is waiting for you to do all the work and then come and get your successes and profits. He's waiting for you to store up good things, and then come and take all of it. The *waster spirit* lets you amass good things for your life and then come to take it.

**I PRAY FOR YOU**: In the Name of Jesus, may God who gives you power to get wealth, also give you Wisdom and power to *keep* it, and enjoy the fruits of your labor, in the Name of Jesus. Amen.

Sickness in the body is a sign that the *waster* is in a person's life. If that is your case, don't say you're falling apart. That is not how you get well. Instead, call your body back in order.

Introject, which is feeling unexplainable movements within your body, is a sign of the *waster spirit* at work.

Sleep attacks such as sleep paralysis, feelings of being choked, or pressed down, or suffocated. You need to call on Jesus. Your only hope in the dream state is to call on Jesus and wake up out of that place in the spirit where you are being oppressed, hurt, or threatened to be killed. And you need to plead the Blood of Jesus.

Call on **JESUS**. Call on Him in the daytime and it will be easier to call on Him at night. Plead the Blood of Jesus.

More signs of the waster:
- Swimming in the dream.
- Sex in dreams with incubus and succubus demons, Lilith, *spirit husbands/wives*. These demons delay or destroy marriages, lives and the hope of marriage and/or the hope of natural children.
- Being pursued in a dream.
- Seeing dead people/ dead relatives in dreams, may also be a sign of family history of occult practices.
- Accidents and mishaps.

If everything feels wrong, often. If it feels as though you are in the wrong place at the wrong time, all the time. If you feel you are in the wrong career or profession, that is the work of the *waster*.

Mixing the world with Christianity; much of the world is into the *occult*. No one will trick God. It is okay to know about things but keep serving God and God only. Also, stay away from festivals that you don't know the **origin** of; most of them honor idol *gods*. It is rather like offering strange fire, before the Lord. If what you are bringing and presenting to the Lord is strange, polluted, or corrupted, even if you've been tricked into doing that, God must destroy what you are bringing to Him. On top of that if He is incensed, then the result will be like Nadab and Abihu.

# Get Delivered from the Waster Spirit:

Thieves of darkness don't just come at night. There are also day wasters.

– that wastes at noonday. Spirit of the waster... (Psalm 91:6)

Thou shalt not be afraid for the destruction that wasteth at noonday. (Psalms 91:5-7)

It is written that God Himself created the *waster* as an instrument to destroy those who want to sin and never repent. God turned the Israelites over to the Midianites and the Amalekites for seven years because they kept sinning. (Judges 6).

Such demons were created to waste lives, talents, gifts, money, relationships, and destinies. If you want to stay in rebellion to God's Word, the *waster* will remain in your life until your life is utterly consumed.

Jesus came so we could be saved. We can repent and receive protection from God and then we would not be *wasted*! You need salvation as a Protestant Christian, not a hodge-podge of religions, false religions, almost-religions and cults mixed together. That will not save you. Actually, it may bring on God's wrath. Mixing religions is playing with fire; it is mocking God. This will get you more trouble than you planned for.

Who you worship determines what fruit you will bear in life. If you don't have any fruit, or the right fruit, you will be cursed. The fig tree was cursed. The prayers in this book (and ministry) are for Protestant Christian and no other *kind*, else the messages and the prayers offered here may make your situation worse than what it already is. God is not mocked.
*"God, I confess that I am a sinner. Please forgive me for the sins I have committed. I repent of all my sins. I believe that Your*

*Son, Jesus Christ, died on the Cross for my sins and rose on the third day. I ask Jesus now to be my Lord and Savior. Please come into my heart, Jesus, and take control of my life. Please fill me and baptize me with Your Holy Spirit. In Jesus' Name, I pray, Amen."*

If you said that prayer, you are now saved and a child of God, in Jesus. Be sure to fully repent, ask for Mercy and then you can wage war against the wasters. If the waster was sent by God, your sorrowful, heartfelt repentance will turn His heart again toward you.

Now, we pray. Don't say you won't do the needed warfare, because that is displeasing to God.

and cursed be he that keepeth back his sword from blood, (Jeremiah 48:10a)

## Waster Fire Prayers

(Some of these prayer points adapted from *Dismantling the Works of the Waster Spirits*, by Apostle Paul A. Williams).

I refuse to be wasted, in the Name of Jesus. Every waster of my prosperity, fall down and die, in the Name of Jesus. Power to fight and win, fall upon my life right now, in the Name of Jesus Christ!

Thunder Fire of God, arise and scatter every power on assignment to waste my life and destiny, in the Name of Jesus Christ!

Powers of darkness operating to destroy my destiny, you are a liar, perish by Fire!!! Die, in the Name of Jesus Christ!

Fire of God, pass through my spirit, soul, and body and burn to ashes every instrument of the wasters at work in my life, in the Name of Jesus Christ!

I command all household wasters, enemies from my own house, by the power in the Blood of Jesus, I terminate all your contracts in my life, in Jesus' Name!

Blood of Jesus arise and dismantle every curse, spell, declaration, and incantation of the wasters over my life, in the Name of Jesus Christ!

Evil covenants made on my behalf, you are cancelled by the Blood of Jesus, in the Name of Jesus Christ!

With the Divine Hammer, I dismantle every satanic altar speaking over my life, in the Name of Jesus Christ!

Foundational *wasters* and *spirits* operating in my life and family, what are you waiting for??? Fall and die, in the Name of Jesus Christ!

By the Blood of Jesus, I erase every evil mark of the wasters made upon my life, in the Name of Jesus Christ!

Fire of God, arise and burn to ashes every coven of darkness assigned to block my blessings, in Jesus's Name!!

By the Thunder Fire of God, I dismantle every satanic assignment to waste my virtues, and blessings, in the Name of Jesus Christ!

Angels of God, slam shut every dimensional access point the *wasters* have been using to access my life so that no man can ever again open them, and that they be hermetically sealed by the Blood of Jesus, in the Name of Jesus Christ! Amen.

I command all the good of my life that was scattered by the wasters to gather up again and be restored into my life, in the Name of Jesus Christ!

# Prayers Against Prosperity Wasters

(Adapted from *Battling the Wasters*, Dr. D.K. Olukoya, Mountain of Fire Ministries)

I release myself from every evil family pattern of poverty, in the Name of Jesus.

My prosperity on every evil altar, I withdraw you now, in the Name of Jesus.

Every *spirit of leaking pockets*, come out with all your roots, by Fire, in Jesus' Name.

Prosperity paralysis from household wickedness, come out with all your roots, and DIE, by Fire, in Jesus' Name.

*Spirit of fragmented life*, come out with all your roots, in Jesus' Name.

*Spirit of debt*, spirit of poverty and all *spirits* that travel with *poverty*, come out with all your roots, and DIE, in Jesus' Name.

Financial or business paralysis by witchcraft, come out with all your roots, in Jesus' Name.

Every wasting, devouring, satanic insect prepared against me, be dissolved by Holy Ghost acid, in the Name of Jesus.

## Fire of God

*From "Warfare Prayers Against the Wasters"*
http://pastormike-spirituallift.blogspot.com/2012/02/warfare-prayers-i-waste-every-waster-of.html

Let the Fire of God answer the fire of the enemy, and let the God that answers by Fire, be God, in the Name of Jesus. (X7)

O Lord, let Your wasters waste my enemies, in the Name of Jesus.

O Lord, release Your Fire to go before me and burn the challengers of my soul, in the Name of Jesus.

Any evil conjured against me, vanish, in the Name of Jesus.

I oppress the wicked, by Fire, in the Name of Jesus.

O Lord, let my divine destiny appear; let every counterfeit destiny disappear, in the Name of Jesus.

I reject all satanic interference and rearrangement of my destiny, in Jesus' Name.

Let the handwriting of household wickedness be blotted out, by the Blood of Jesus.

O Lord, send divine plagues upon my Pharaoh, in the Name of Jesus.

Every power trying to remove my name from the mind of my helpers, fall down and die, in the Name of Jesus.

I crush every satanic lion rising against my success, in the Name of Jesus.

O Lord, let Your mighty voice thunder against my enemies and throw them into confusion, in the Name of Jesus.

Let every satanic ambush be frustrated, in the Name of Jesus.

Every virtue of my life that the enemy is sitting on, come back to me, come back to me, come back to me by Fire, in the Name of Jesus.

Anything planted into my life to disgrace me, come out now, in the Name of Jesus.

God's people shall never be ashamed, in the Name of Jesus.

No weapon that is formed against thee shall prosper, and every tongue that rises against me, I shall condemn. I condemn the *waster spirit*, by the Fire in the Blood of Jesus. (X5)

I condemn every tongue that has come against me, in the Name of Jesus.

## In the Name of Jesus

Every aggression against my prosperity, be paralyzed, in the Name of Jesus.

My blessings shall not stagnate, in the Name of Jesus.

Spirit of lack, come out with all your roots, in the Name of Jesus.

Spirit of insufficiency, come out with all your roots, in the Name of Jesus.

Spirit of not enough in time or on time, come out with all your roots, in Jesus' Name.

Every *spirit of delay*, especially in finances, come out with all your roots, in the Name of Jesus.

Every satanic bird, insect, or animal prepared against me, be disintegrated by Fire, in the Name of Jesus.

*(The above prayers were adapted from Evangelist Joshua Orekhie. The prayers below adapted from DK Olukoya.)*

Users of charms, collapse by the power in the Blood of Jesus, in the Name of Jesus.

Every witchcraft power disturbing my progress, die, in the Name of Jesus.

Every occultic power disturbing my progress, Die, in the Name of Jesus.

My Father, disgrace the human beings that are working with Satan to trouble my life, in the Name of Jesus.

My Father, disgrace the human beings that are working with Satan to destroy Your purposes in my life, in the Name of Jesus. (X3)

Any power drawing my blood—vomit it, and DIE, in the Name of Jesus.

Any power that has tasted my blood, you will not stop vomiting until you confess it and then DIE, in the Name of Jesus.

Lord, let your powers fall upon me afresh, in the Name of Jesus.

Wasting powers of my father's house, DIE, in the Name of Jesus.

Powers of the wasters, I waste you now, in the Name of Jesus.

Powers of the waster working against my career, calling, family, marriage, business, success, education, children, DIE, in the Name of Jesus.

Thank You, Jesus. X3

Powers chasing away my customers, clients, business connections, DIE, in the Name of Jesus.

I bind every *spirit* of bad investment, in the Name of Jesus.

Every power on assignment to cause me to make poor business decisions, fail and and die, in the Name of Jesus.

Every curse pronounced against my finances and spiritual growth, BREAK, in the Name of Jesus.

Desert power, barrenness, you are a liar, DIE, in the Name of Jesus.

Let mine outcasts dwell with thee, Moab; be thou a covert to them from the face of the waster. For the extortioner is at an end, the wasting hath ceased, the oppressors are consumed out of the land. (Isaiah 16:4).

For the extortioner is at an end, the wasting hath ceased, the oppressors are consumed out of the land. God's people shall not be ashamed, in the Name of Jesus. (Joel 2:26)

I seal this word, these decrees and declarations across every realm, every dimension, age, era, timeline, past, present, and future, to infinity, in the Name of Jesus, by the Blood of Jesus and the Holy Spirit of Promise, in the Name of Jesus.

The *spirit of retaliation* is a waster.

When you are pursuing God's will, and your destiny from God, the enemy will send retaliation against you to "waste" your blessings, potential, opportunities, resources, helpers, promotions, or anything that had been designed to be a steppingstone towards your future and your destiny. Retaliation is a waster, and therefore, any attacks because of these prayers, backfire 7X against the sender, in the Name of Jesus.

*Amen.*

## Recovery: Take It Back

Fight against the demonic force called the *waster*, then begin praying for restoration on all that has been stolen, devoured, or wasted in your life.

> But if he is caught, he must pay back seven times what he stole, even if he has to sell everything in his house.
> (Proverbs 6:31)

Fight to take your life back. God has spoken in the above verse. Have you appropriated the promises of God? Have you prayed, decreed, and declared those things into existence, or back into your life?

The Spirit leads us to pray for what we need; He even makes intercession for us (Romans 8:26). If God promised it, then it is so. GOD does not dangle carrots before us. If we are in God and pursue the promises of God, the Word says that we should not be ashamed, or come to shame, in the Name of Jesus.

**My people shall never be ashamed. (Joel 2:26)**

The devil comes to steal, kill, and destroy; he *wastes* blessings, provisions, and opportunities that God prepares for us.

God hates waste and He hates anyone who wastes His people. I command all the good of my life that has been scattered by the *wasters* to gather together again, and be restored to me, in Jesus' Name.

I decree: I recover all, (X3). I recover everything in my life that was lost to the *wasters*, I recover it all, seven-fold, in Jesus' Name. Lord, restore the years, redeem the time, in the Name of Jesus. **AMEN.**

## Dear Reader

Thank you for acquiring and reading this volume. May you take up your warfare and fight! Defeat every wicked plan and action of the waster spirit, in the Name of Jesus.

May you recover all, in the Name of Jesus.

Amen.

*Dr. Marlene Miles*

## Other books by this author

AK: The Adventures of the Agape Kid

AMONG SOME THIEVES

Ancestral Powers

Barrenness, *Prayers Against*

Battlefield of Marriage, *The*

Beauty Curses, *Warfare Prayers Against*

Behave

Blindsided: *Has the Old Man Bewitched You?*

https://a.co/d/5O2fLLR

Churchzilla, The Wanna-Be, Supposed-to-be Bride of Christ

Collective Captivity, *Break Free From*

Courts of Marriage: Prayers for Marriage in the Courts of Heaven (prayerbook)

Courtroom Warfare @ Midnight (prayerbook)

Curses of Blind Men

Demonic Cobwebs (prayerbook)

Demonic Time Bombs

Demons Hate Questions

Devil Loves Trauma, *The*

Devil Weapons: Unforgiveness, Bitterness,…

The Devourers: *Thieves of Darkness* (Book 4)

Do Not Swear by the Moon

Don't Refuse Me, Lord (4 book series)

Dream Defilement

The Emptiers: *Thieves of Darkness* (Book 1)

Every Evil Bird

Evil Touch

Failed Assignment

Family Token (*forthcoming*)

Fantasy Spirit Spouse

FAT Demons (The): *Breaking Demonic Curses*

The Fold (5 book series)

The Fold (Book 1)

Name Your Seed (Book 2)

The Poor Attitudes of Money (3)

Do Not Orphan Your Seed (4)

For the Sake of the Gospel (5)

Fruit of the Womb:

Gates of Thanksgiving

Gathered

got HEALING? Verses for Life

got LOVE? Verses for Life

got HOPE? Verses for Life

got money?

How to Dental Assist

How to Dental Assit2: Be Productive, Not Wasteful

I Take It Back

Legacy

Let Me Have A Dollar's Worth

Level the Playing Field

Living for the NOW of God

Lose My Location https://a.co/d/crD6mV9

Man Safari, *The*

Marriage Ed. Rules of Engagement & Marriage

Made Perfect in Love

Money Hunters: Beware of Those

Motherboard (The) - soul prosperity series

Name Your Seed

Occupy: *Until I Return*

Plantation Souls

Players Gonna Play

Power Money: Nine Times the Tithe

The Power of Wealth *(forthcoming)*

Powers Above

Marriage Ed.: Rules of Engagement & Marriage

Mulberry Tree, *The* https://a.co/d/6JP7KqK

Seasons of Grief

Seasons of Waiting

Seasons of War

Second Marriage, Third--, Any Marriage

Sift You Like Wheat

Spirits of Death, Hell & the Grave, Pass Over Me and My House

Soul Prosperity soul prosperity series 3

https://a.co/d/5p8YvCN

Souls Captivity soul prosperity series 2

The Spirit of Poverty

StarStruck

SUNBLOCK

The Swallowers: Thieves of Darkness (Book 3)
https://a.co/d/d5PfloB

Take It Back https://a.co/d/dZnVE25

This Is NOT That: How to Keep Demons from Coming at You

Throne of Grace: Courtroom Prayer

Time Is of the Essence

Too Many Wives: *Why You Have Lady Problems*

**Tormenting Spirits**
https://a.co/d/dAogEJf

Toxic Souls

Triangular Power *(series)*

    Powers Above

    SUNBLOCK

    Do Not Swear by the Moon

    STARSTRUCK

Uncontested Doom

Unguarded House, *The*

Unseen Life, *The* (forthcoming)

Upgrade: How to Get Out of Survival Mode

    Toxic Souls (Book 2 of series)

    Legacy (Book 3 of series)

Warfare Prayer Against Beauty Curses

Warfare Prayer Against Poverty

The Wasters: Thieves of Darkness (Book 2)

What Have You to Declare? What Do You Have With You from Where You've Been?

When I Was A Child, I Prayed As a Child

When the Devourer is Rebuked

The Wilderness Romance https://a.co/d/jfkMlnj

- The Social Wilderness
- The Sexual Wilderness
- The Spiritual Wilderness

The Wilderness Romance series is not a romance novel series. These books are about relationships with people who are still in the Wilderness, how to avoid them, or what to do if you've married one.

## Series:

### The Fold (a series on Godly finances)
https://a.co/d/4hz3unj

### Soul Prosperity Series https://a.co/d/bz2M42q

## Thieves of Darkness series

## Triangular Powers https://a.co/d/aUCjAWC

## Upgrade (series) *How to Get Out of Survival Mode* https://a.co/d/aTERhXO

www.ingramcontent.com/pod-product-compliance
Lightning Source LLC
Chambersburg PA
CBHW060846050426
42453CB00008B/860